T0380781

A Stir
of Echoes
From Verses
PAST

Don Simmons a.k.a. Don Poetiq

Print information available on the last page

Rev. date: 07/01/2019

To order additional copies of this book, contact:
Xlibris
1-888-795-4274
www.Xlibris.com
Orders@Xlibris.com

Dedication

This book is dedicated to my Lord, and Savior Jesus Christ.
Without the adversity in my life.
And, without the Grace, and Mercy
you freely gave to get me through it.
All this would not be possible.
May the words, which you help me to evince on paper
do their part to effect change in any place you may send them.
And, please Lord, continue to mold me in your furnace.
So that I may be a vessel of honor that you may use for your glory.

ACKNOWLEDGEMENTS

Poetry is the soundtrack of life

—by Don Simmons

I would like to take this time to recognize those who influenced me either negatively, or positively. Without each one of these people, and the events that they're tied to. This book would not exist . . .

My teachers at P.S. 45 K. Ms. Erin. Ms. Teller. Ms. Anduz, and Ms. Mercer. Mr. Spaulding. Mr. Cohen. Mr.Rosen. Mr. Covington. Mr. Hairston, and Mr. Wilbeck(Who in particular taught how tragic it would be if a teacher suddenly decided to quit because they felt underappreciated. An extra special thanks goes to Mrs. Susan Zatt, who understood, loved, and respected me when I had no idea as to what understanding, love, and respect were. We didn't part the best of friends. Still, if it is axiomatic that "Time heals all wounds". I hope that the ones that I inflicted have long since been made well. I was just a child. Please forgive me.

To Mrs. Spieser. I remember the concern you showed towards me. I thank you from the deepest part of my heart.

Mr. Fimano, Mr. Commaducci, and Mr. Callas. You guys always seemed like cops. But, you were really stand up human beings.

To Mr. Goldberg, Mr. Zatt, Mr. Perazzo, Mr. Stolz, Mr. Dubose, P.O. Mulligan. And, to any teacher, or staff member who imparted a word of kindness . . . Thank you.

To childhood friends, and acquaintances. Glen, and Melvin Moore. Jacob Ayers. Pucho (Alberto Morales). The whole Morales family. The Polite family. The Ashe family. Lisa Ates (R.I.P.). Valerie, Fern, Paulette, Evelyn Rodriguez. Anna, Lisa Greg, Anita, Samantha, and Sandra Gladden. Darlene, Jeffery(Jazzy Jeff) and Eric Williams. Madeline Rosado.

To Red. His brother Dice(R.I.P)

To Ms.Todd, Mr. Eaton, and Jimmy. The Lutheran Church Of Our Savior, and all past members. To Juan.

To the Evangelists of 8001 State Road in PA. Brother Stewart, who first told me about Christ!

To Julian Coward, and Dwight King. Two of the most intelligent people I have ever had the pleasure of meeting.

To Fudge, Guy, Andrew Freire, Zaki, and Melvin Owens (aka Mel in, and out Big Dog!).

To Mr. Hudson, whose own arduous journey is much more significant than my own. May you find Peace, Comfort, and the Streets! Ricky Brillion . . . In The Name Of Jesus we have the victory! Desmond Blake(aka Mr. Principle) Thanks for caring.

To Reverend Boston, and Reverend Duane Smith. To the New York Theological Seminary, and its staff.

To those who gave me instruction behind the wall. Bruce, Woody, Johnny, Khalil, Greeneyes, and Saladin Muhammed (R.I.P. my brother). Dr. Webber, Dr. Vernoy. To Caroline, Tamara, Dana, Tracy, Louise, Mia, Christine, Ferne, Donald, Vilma, Christopher, Rodney, and Dr. Dobesh. Mrs. Ford, and all the other nurses, doctors, and staff who made my stay at NYP Cornell Weill bearable. I always keep my promises. To Joseph, Randy, Donna, Sheree, Leslie, et al at the Bridge Program . . . Peace. To Emily, Aldo, Arnie, Bob, Steve, and all the other Scrabble players in Washington Square Park. Especially to Herb, whose compassion, and assistance got me through some pretty tough times. I can't say thank you enough. LionHeart, Joey, Transit P.O. Big Red, who used to carry an ax handle. Sgt. Reyes (6th Precinct). Divine(Michael Galbraith). Sammy/Rebecca Henry Tilo. To all of the forgotten children past, and present of 42st. I'm always and forever one of Midnight's Children. Trini, and Anthony Price(aka Locust), To all the talented artists I've met over the course of my life. Ned Williams. Mr. Alvin Ailey(R.I.P.). Kamal Edwards. James Johnson. Infinite, and Amir. Face, Rock, and Qua from Greenhaven. Brother Bey. The most eloquent, sincere, and thought provoking poet I have ever met. May your fame one day be commensurate to your immense talent. The Miller family. R.I.P. Hattie. The Malik Pharmacy.

Peace Amir. Vernon Capps, Nova Daniels, Derek Baines . . . God is love, and in Him is no darkness. Mr. Lombardi. Mr. Glen Johnson. Dr, Zeverin Emagalit(which means wagon in Teso). Mrs Patricia Adams. And, to all the other professors at Duchess Community College. Jose(aka Deadeye R.I.P.). Marcus. To Bobby Van Doren Smith, who was one of the first people to instill in me the importance of vocabulary. Mr. Kenji Hara from Japan.Ruth Felix, and family. Carmen Beltre, and family. Darlene. All the poets who ripped it at the Nuyorican.

Dream, Vandanal, Shayla, Ainsley Burrows, Nathan P, Ruby K(one of the illest poets white, black, or other).

You've always been there for me brother. You're forever in my heart. The Village Underground. The Bowery Poet's club. Mr. K Lamonte, and Solomon's Porch. Mr, John Mcdonagh from the Doneagal Clan in Ireland.

Danny, Mike, Anthony, and Pedro . . . The D.O. To my mom, dad, sister, brother, brother in law, nephews, cousins, and numerous aunts and uncles. I don't have to write much . . . You know what you mean to me. And, you know what our journey has been like. If I forgot anybody, please forgive me. I'll get you next time . . .

Where Then Can Love Be Found?

A place where hatred is taken captive, and joyous laughter will resound.
But, people are devoid of understanding . . . Where Then Can Love Be Found?

We're living in the Final Days; days of darkness and confusion.
Through the Beast, False Prophet, AntiChrist . . . The Masters Of Illusion.

I see a land that cries for Justice, a world where evil roams.
I see Warfare, Pain, and Emaciation . . . The Elderly Left Alone.

Search deeply within your beings, why have we reached this lost condition?
Where are our lives are now uncertain . . . nonexistent apparitions.

Who can we blame for all the tragedy; where can we go to find a cure?
The solution is not beyond us, only Love can make life pure.

Many nations have great problems, several countries overseas.
Yet, take a look, decode the cipher . . . They're killing minorities.

Our children, precious little ones, in recent years their hopes have waned.
They've been shot down, abused, neglected; each human shares in the blame.

In New York City something appalling, a day of shameful doom.
A mother had a child ripped from her belly . . . A Seed No Chance To Bloom.

Love is cloaked in elusive mystery; carnal man cannot obtain.
It can only be found if you Cleanse your Spirits/ yes, its meaning is quite arcane.

It's Unconditional, Very Humble, looks not on Race or Color.
And, I doubt very seriously you know its worth, if you can't even Love your Brother.

I know we can reach the apogee, so Break the Chains and don't be bound.
Still, until that day, I'll ask a question . . . Where Then Can Love Be Found?

A Few More Burdens To Bear

There's tribulation, but also triumph, one day no more despair.
If we just can reach tomorrow . . . A Few More Burdens To Bear.

I see chaos and people lanquishing, no unity amongst the races.
Society's countenance has been dimmed; the lack of hope etched on their faces.

I met a child who said "Don't worry, I'm not sad because I'm poor . . .
My father's in prison, my brother's a dealer . . . my mother is just a whore."

Deceit and Avarice, ignoble actions; Equal Justice for all denied.
Where can I go to find some solace? . . . For, these problems are nationwide.

Turn on the t.v. and see the violence, hard luck stories in all the papers.
Crime's miasma has left us flummoxed . . . Rightwing Bombings and Baby Rapers.

Children of the world are dying quickly, yes, many elegies daily sung.
Life has dealt them a mortal blow . . . Man, why did Tupac die so young?

In every ghetto a broken spirit, unstable families are ripped asunder.
Will all of these burdens bring forth an answer/with many tears I often wonder.

Still, beyond the scope of conflict, for better days a light is shining.
When Peace and Love will destroy the Beast . . . and this system of his designing.

I wish this poem to induce a pathos, words so poignant they make you cry.
But, let your core absorb the essence, or its truth will pass you by.

These trying times seem insurmountable with all of the sorrows we have to share.
Until The Highest Plane is reached . . . . A Few More Burdens To Bear.

New York City . . . . Vicious Cycle

Pushed to the edge by reality, yes, these verses will stifle.

A revolving door always present; New York City . . . . Vicious Cycle.

This is a poem about the hardships, and monotony of this age

The world unchanging in its essence . . . . many problems to assuage.

Why is our purlieu in such predicaments, the morass so intense?

It seems the fire has been extinguished; in other words we've acquiesced.

Hallways, alleys, subway stations/where the weak and troubled roam.

Considered dross by our society, that's why the streets became their home.

Our youth in dire straits, how can they be redeemed?

High school dropouts, teenage suicide, and for crack my brother's fiend,

Homeless people are anathema; we seldom love the poor.

New York City . . . Vicious Cycle . . . . where daily living is abhorred.

A nimbus cloud, can't see the acme/ Where Then Can Love Be Found?

The cacophony breaks the silence; the voice of weeping does resound.

Welfare parents in a quandary, just barely scraping by.

Elderly people doing no better . . . though receiving S.S.I.

New York City . . . . Vicious Cycle, spreading like a deadly cancer.

Minority children disenfranchised; drug dealing is their answer.

Boys and girls, young and pretty/ jailbait, nowhere to run.

A perfect target for a pedophile; their tender lives have just begun.

Dark specters in every borough; people lost and living trifle.

Eight million stories, naked truth . . . New York City . . . Vicious Cycle.

The Fire That Burned Their Souls

They searched for Love and Understanding, just to fill the empty holes.
Instead of these they found destruction . . . The Fire That Burned Their Souls.

No Light for Midnight's Children, some died while in their teens.
Just close your eyes and feel my words as I limn with vivid scenes.

On "Broadway" there was a "Playland", more succinct a big arcade . . .
Where "Chicken hawks" espied the quarry, and the lives of youth would fade.

These kids allured by empty promises, of money hope and better care.
Yet, angels cry in the empyrean for the boys of Times Square.

Selling their bodies, passed around, in sordid acts they engaged.
Tossed to and fro by life's tempest . . . precious young ones underage.

Vitiated while tender, an early death was their fame.
So many gamins gone forever, I even knew some by name.

Turned out and beaten daily, yet, I remember him fondly . . .
A child whore with no egress; his street appellation was "Blondie".

The old tricks called him "Dead Eye", his right lid badly sagged.
But, he was Warm, Kind, and Innocent . . . never argued or bragged.

His young ashes now scattered, another Dream blown away.
A misnomer now righted for my late friend "Jose".

"Down In The Zero", sweet whispers, yes, I still hear their voice.
They found rest in eternity from a life without choice.

So , bow your heads, show them homage, for they have paid heavy tolls.
At "Heavens Gate" there is forgiveness . . . from The Fire That Burned Their Souls.

Ten Different Shades Of Gray

Ten Different Shades Of Gray, this poem explains my world.
Just variations of my sadness, a lonely little girl.

My father visits me every night, my hidden flower has been broken.
I've been left alone to suffer, yes by a love verboten.

Daddy's daughter, prepubescent; a kid who must endure.
My heart is clean, devoid of guile/why must I live my life impure?

Yet, I'm treated like the plague, just like a poisoned tumor.
Shameful whispers, schoolmates talking . . . everyone has heard the rumor.

I even told my mother "I'm being molested!" she just regarded me with scorn.
Ten Different Shades Of Gray . . . she said I led my father on.

Yes, my momma has forsaken me, and won't even say my name.
Can't you see I'm just a child; who'll help to ease my pain?

I had no choice but to kill my father, a tortured soul has been relieved.
Stolen innocence has no cure, maybe now they will believe!

Still, I'm pregnant, haunting nightmares, I can't articulate my gloom.
No doubt my son will be my brother . . . ill born progeny in my womb.

Left alone in his affliction, he will be a bastard twice.
Who's his papa, what's the answer? . . . conceived through sin and vice.

The boy I have will be an outcast, and surely be despised.
But, everyone will know the truth, because he'll have my daddy's eyes.

I know a girl, whose life was similar, so respects I have to pay.
Her father touched her, but denied it . . . **Ten Different Shades Of Gray.**

Metaphor

I was several miles away . . .
in a nondescript neighborhood
of the city

Many people, who now donate
money to a certain fund
because it's trendy/encountered me
that day and did nothing

I was Hurt, Hungry, and Afraid

Yet, no one lifted a hand
to help me/My clothes were worn,
I needed some sleep/school wasn't even
an option . . .

Too young to be caught up
in such a turbulent sandstorm

But, the winds came
and carried the uncaring
multitudes right past me

My suffering was so complete,
that the wind, which propelled others
into stagnant motion
gave me no comfort at all . . .

. . . For, people often do
bad things to me . . . .

I get Molested, Raped,
Abused/and left to starve
in basements . . . just like
my brother Faheem

So, everything in and around me
becomes callused—when innocence
can no longer be seen in my eyes

What good is being a desert flower,
when nobody knows of my beauty
except for me?

How does this sprig, which only grows
in a barren wasteland continue to be?

Because God smiles on the defenseless,
and sends His Life Giving Water
to resurrect this dying plant

Still, I often have to prostitute myself,
just to survive in this wilderness
I call my home

Amongst the other unwanted cacti

. . . Who am I? . . .

. . . . A neglected child
in the inner-city . . . .

Forsaken, Lost, and never Loved

. . . . Alone in a place where
nobody knows my name . . . .

. . . Ground Zero . . .

Gestapo

It was approximately 4 in the morning—
No different from any other day in a Third World Country . . .

I was walking that morning through Tiannamen Square . . .

When I caught sight of something that made me stop
on a dime

Within a plexiglass enclosure, on the main floor of the square/
there were many people seated

Most were neatly dressed and looked to have some sort
of purpose for being there . . .

Then there were the dissidents - tattered clothing -
unkempt hair - soiled faces - and worn shoes

These were the ones singled out
by the gestapo . . .

. . . simply because they were resting . . .

The gestapo were menacing

17 shots/tight black gloves/
and pepper spray

Each person who was sleeping . . . . who looked
different from the Mainstream - was promptly set upon by the gestapo
They were surrounded by the gestapo, and the
aggressive aura which emanated from them

I couldn't hear the words that were exchanged

But, because I was viewing this encounter from
outside the box, and had witnessed it up close many times before . . .
. . . I knew that the gestapo's words weren't soothing or pleasant

Each innocent evildoer who didn't have the proper
papers for passage to somewhere was asked to leave the enclosure

Sickened by what I saw, I turned and began to
walk away . . .

And, immediately, these words blared from a public
address system: The Amtrak to Trenton is now boarding
at gate three

No . . . I wasn't in Tiannamen Square/I wasn't even
in a quote - unquote Third World Country

I was right at Penn Station/watching the police
carry out their acts of terrorism against the homeless

. . . Just like the terrorism that takes place overseas . . .

. . . So much for Democracy and the American Way . . .

. . .

Why?

Why are children beaten and maimed?
Why are black men imprisoned when framed?
Why do the poor live each day with a sigh?
Why are we born, grow old, and just die?

Why do we backstab, betray a true friend?
Why does the rain from heaven descend?
So many people are wealthy, then why is there lack?
Why is everything evil equated with BLACK?

We say children are our future/ a glory divine
Then why Conyers Georgia? and why Columbine?

Between the young and the old a generational gap
Why do we scorn and misunderstand rap?
We have Love for the Lord, and frown on abortion
Why does corporate America engage in extortion?

Once prayers guided schools, now it seems it's too late
Why separation between Churches and State?
Divided we fall and united we stand . . .
So, why does Great Africa exist by a strand?

The Land Of The Free, in our lore it's been told
Yet, now there's few rainbows and even less pots of gold

All the signs are before us, yet our vision stays blurred
Why believe a False Prophet instead of God's Word?

The AntiChrist, Beast, and Babylon's Whore
Why Osama Bin Laden and rumors of war?

I'm groping in darkness for answers, with no concrete reply
So, I'll continue my sojourn with the question of . . .

. . . Why? . . .

But, The Birds No Less Will Sing

With worldwide stress and paranoia, what will tomorrow bring?
Yes, sunlit skies have turned to darkness . . . But, The Birds No Less Will Sing.

Evil things are now unfolding, the thirty third mason degree . . .
The faith of many has all but left them, from fearful sights their eyes will see.

Suicide bombings, Islamic Jihad/they have allah as their guide.
Capitalist gains which makes them poorer/this is the reason that we're despised.

A crazy president who's high off power, what the hell is this man thinking?
Yet, in his home he's not respected . . . he cannot curb his daughter's drinking.

Disgruntled youth with rage and sadness, beware the "Children Of The Corn."
Negligent parents, abuse, bad schooling, misunderstanding, and kiddie porn.

Homosexual priests, the pope condones it, God's Word they're not obeying.
Behind their collars, the trust is minimal; they now stalk the child who's praying.

AIDS, MAD COW, there's SARS, EBOLA, and oh yeah the WEST NILE VIRUS.
The Queen Of Heaven and pagan rituals . . . for some their god's Osiris.

Since 911 we're strapped for money, you can almost hear the market crash.
In some countries they sell their organs/while others sift through landfill trash.

Collective sighs from every nation, we have to hold our breath to cope.
Still, birds will sing outside your window, and what that means my friends is hope.

Our societal fabric is left in tatters, from salted tears all eyes will sting.
Prodigious problems, and few solutions . . . But, The Birds No Less Will Sing.

The Reunion Of Heaven And Man

Forgotten
Asians
Languishing
Under
Nefarious

Despots
Asking
For
Answers

You who call yourselves the children of Buddha/How is it
that I being a Westerner can understand what you cannot?

For, I clearly see the 8 Jings and 5 directions
manifested in Falun Gong

I can hear their silent exhalation of 36 breaths
descending into the Tan Tien . . .

I can taste the uric acid which seeps through their pores/
because they have mastered the the Iron Thread technique
of Hung Gar— boiling the water to obtain its steam . . .

Yin palm over Yang palm/a folding of the legs . . .
Perfect Lotuses cut down before they've had
a chance to blossom into eternity

It's sin enough you kill the men!

The fairer sex, I wonder why?/Since Chairman Mao
once made a statement, "Women hold up half the sky."

I try to fathom your motivations behind this blatant form
of Self Genocide

Yes, I would gladly empty my cup to taste your tea

Still, the tea of your understanding is not edifying,
or nourishing/It is like Wormwood, which destroys the purity
of the Urogenital Diaphragm

This poison has risen up to enter
through your right ventricle . . .

Clogging your heart with Bad Blood/so that you are no longer
able to think or act humanely

Traditional Chinese Medicine can do nothing
to correct your diseased meridian of hatred

Sickness of the spirit can only be cured by allowing
your Ni wan to absorb the heavenly energy of The "Son"

For, the Path that holds your redemption . . . .

. . . . Is Eightfold . . .

. . . The Enlightment Of Falun Dafa . . .

The Vision

I was standing on the sand of the sea shore, thinking about
a recent catastrophe/ when suddenly/darkness closed in
like the shadows of twilight/ Saddened by the enormity of
of it all/ a trail of tears trickled down my face . . .

That's when the hand of the Almighty gently lifted me above
the shore, and asked me in a voice like rushing waters . . .

Son Of Man/what do you see? . . .

I see an ocean of crack vials, automatic weapons/and blackened
prison cells with white backgrounds

a palpable silence ensued

Son Of Man/what do you see? . . .

I see waves of murdered children, and not one of them is a teen/
from Lisa Steinberg, Meagan Konka, little Amber, and
Sabrina Green . . .

What else do you see? . . .

I see two men walking hand and hand . . .

The first man is one of great stature/on his forehead is an engraved word

. . . Deceiver . . .

I see him stretching out his right hand as if beckoning the whole world to him

In the palm of his hand I see the number Thirty Three and a Third

. . . Drops Of Blood Dripped From That Hand . . .

Within those drops of blood/ I see two towers falling to the earth . . .

And, countless soldiers dying/trying to defend Iraqi Oil Fields . . .

. . . I see global hunger, tainted Stem Cells . . . hands raised to heaven; a desperate plea . . .

I see Seven Plagues before The Judgement . . . and Super Strains of H.I.V.

The peace that I felt throughout the vision was temporarily taken from my spirit . . .

But, the Lord was never far from me/just a prayer away . . .

I then saw a colossal Dragon open its mouth/a great flood issued forth . . .

. . . And a question came from eternity . . .

Son Of Man/what do you see now?

I answered/I see all the ghettos of suffering . . .

And that's when I realized that this catastrophe doesn't happen once in a while

. . . It happens everyday . . .

. . . A Tsunami . . .

Hemmed In Every Side

So many things are about to happen; few places that
you can hide.

New World Order, Disease, and Violence . . .
Hemmed In On Every Side.

Prisoner, Outcast, Loser; these sorbriquets
have made me small.

Yet, through Grace I've been illumined/
Babylon will surely fall.

I only write through the Holy Spirit; from
on High it has been Spoken.

Heaven and earth are fleeting entities,
but God's Truth cannot be broken . . .

On The Scroll it was decreed, I must
evince what it reveals.

. . . Christ The King Alone Was Worthy To Unloose The Seven Seals . . .

The first few Seals spoke of destruction, as Four
Horsemen began ride.

They slew with Famine, Sword, and Hatred . . .
Hemmed In On Every Side.

Beneath The Alter Souls Were Crying; for The
Word they had been slain.

Their Righteous Blood would be avenged,
for, their deaths were not in vain.
A Mighty Earthquake, The Sun Was Darkened,
then The Sky Began To Fold.

Verses 12 and 13 of Chapter Six . . .
In Revelation These Things Fortold.

Israel's Children, The Scattered Remnant;
from their lips came forth a song.

They are Redeemed, First Fruits, and Virgins . . .
One Hundred and Forty Four Thousand Strong.

Later on their was a Woman, and Her raiment
was The Sun.

She bore a Child who held the Scepter;
Spiritual Warfare had begun.

Its grievous wound was quickly healed,
The world looked on with great surprise.

Seven Heads, Ten Horns, and Blasphemy . . .
. . . In The End The Beast Will Rise.

No doubt this Crucible is the last; Love
And Hate Will Now Collide.

Let all The Saints put on their Armor . . .

. . . Hemmed In On Every Side . . .

E.T.

. . . . A shrill whistle pierced my midnight cognitions/ . . .
. . . and a grotesque body, which once had life was
pulled from the past

It had been submerged several days
in a river aboil from the summer heat

Severely decomposed/"55" memories

The head was cruelly bloated
and deformed

Where an eye should have been/a dark hollow cavern

No hair
No nose . . . holes in various places

This sight was laid under glass
with a long pillow,and enclosed in
metal/then the throngs came to see this
horrific spectacle

That's when the hideous, unrecognizable
mass that I initiallly saw changed and
emerged from the transparent coffin . . .

. . . It was a young boy . . .

At first he did nothing, except stand there
while tears streamed down his face

Then, as if trying to say something/he
parted his lips . . .

I could smell the rot of the racism
which murdered this child, and realized why I was
plagued with this vision . . . .

. . . Because even though my physical was at rest . . .
my mind refused to fall asleep to the history which
shaped my blackness

Meanwhile, the conscious of many remain
"Eyes Wide Shut"

. . . . The Spirit Of Emmit Till, still cries
out to be remembered . . .

F.O.T.W

There he is again/searching . . .
for me—the object of his disdain/
his bete noire

Looking at him through the facets of my vision . . .
—He is a hulking one of them

The ones who seek to cut off my already
truncated life

Swish! a swift and practiced mano
takes aim

Lo Mein from last night's relvelry
my launch to escape

. . . . too evasive . . .

Yet, my aggravation is apparent—
if only to myself

Agitated setae sit stilly upon a
bottled back

Nonetheless, I take this latest attack
in stride . . . . An insignificant setback in this
current battle between he and I/between I
and them

Since this is a constant struggle/one that has
probably been going on since the inception of time . . .

I profoundly ponder past assaults from
whilom ages

Is this the Genocide that my brothers from
another phylum speak of through the whisper mill?
For, I am also Black, but very
uncomely/I am Black, but the sun
has not made me so . . .

No! . . .

I have attained my shape, size, and melanin
through the evolutionary hand of creation

Still. do I deserve to procreate,
to be fruitful and multiply?

Each day my numbers diminish
and nobody questions why?

Yet, every attempt to exterminate my existence
is met with a well executed jete

Since hardly anyone is successful the first time

I then let the momemtum carry me high
and away/until I once again become a
negroid speck on a drab canvas

. . . . A canvas that only I can bring color to . . .

. . . F.O.T.W? . . .

Fly On The Wall

The Monster That Dwells Amongst Us

I have walked the earth's circumference since centuries past   Invented from the imagination of a young girl—a "Novel" scientist gave me life. An amalgam of parts sutured together to form a hideous whole   . Did he?/ Did they?, really believe that my scars could be hidden from the world. Nonetheless, hidden I became/ not because I was locked away in a laboratory   But, because I could never reveal myself to those who would not accept me

. . . .

So, I began to kill, with the brain of the murderer/ criminal I was grafted from. Still, I can speak, think, and articulate just as well as any human that was formed by God . . .

I won't be given a chance though/ because "Brainwash Education"- Rockerfeller Laws—and Racial Profiling/ forever relegate me to the shadow lands of every inner—city . . .

. . . .

I can savor the sweet frangrance of a flower
I am one with the tranquility of a lake
I can see the innocent beauty of a child

. . . .

Yet, every time I show the goodness that is within me
to humanity—I am rejected

. . . and chased inexorably with torches . . .

through the slums and ghettos of a maker,
who only mentions my name in whispers . . .

. . . The creator who made me is society . . .

The Monster I became? . . .

. . . Frankenstein . . .

PARADOX

Anger-What is it?
What color is it?
And, what can we liken it to?

Is the thing that we feel before counting to ten?
Or is it why many Buddhists reflect in Zazen?
Could it be White?
Like the Pillar of Salt that became of Lot's Wife?

Was is **BLACK** like the **Glove of Geronimo Pratt?**
Or Silver like the Bullets that laid Amadou flat?

The blue of uniforms of those who Protect and who Serve?
Maybe the pigment of a person who killed a sick perv
Shaded Brown like the Projects with no hope/ locked inside?
Welfare Yellow like Cheese when you're stripped of your pride

Surely it's the Green of Saudi Arabia's flag
New York gray like the beggar who's treated like slag?

Actually, it isn't manifested in colors
Nor can it be defined
Go now
Entertain what I've said
Remembering the Paradox is that we claim to see RED

The Road That Led To Nowhere

It was a "Worn Path" inside of a prison . . .

Everyone called that path "The Walkway"

Five years and eight months I traversed that walkway.
In the daytime, and only by reason of sunlight did that walkway,
which led to nowhere seem happier.

There were many places that one could go on that walkway.
The RMU with its dismal ambience . . .

It also contained a morgue, for those who had died without
family, without friends . . . and without dignity.

A big building further down, which was always alive with activity/
That was the most important building . . .
An education could be found there . . .
But, most times, that building was just like that walkway/a
place that people went to, yet, its true significance was never fully realized.

Another edifice known as The Main lie several feet ahead.
Its central feature was the commissary/mostly for those who had
to prove to others how much money they didn't have.
Oh, before you got there though, you had to pass the State
Shop/where new outfits of captivity were handed out.

. . . But, no matter which way you decided to go in on that
walkway, whether up or down/ you always came to a cul de sac . . .
A place that let you know that you could go no further.

I remember the many nights I looked down that walkway, which seemed
to be God forsaken . . .
I could see the desolation, suffering, and years of those who had
come before me/and of those who would come after.

. . . Sometimes I saw a solitary C.O.

Was he as affected by being on that walkway as I was by
staring down it?

Or had he somehow become obdurate and incapable of feeling?

Maybe in his lifetime he had never come across "The Road Less Traveled"

So, that was his Green Mile/ to lead a sad, monotonous existence
which never changed.

Even though that C.O. was probably in misery . . . he couldn't even
bring himself to have empathy towards us/ even though us
prisoners trod the same lonely walkway as he.

. . . One morning while I went down that walkway, I encountered
a fork on the left hand side.

. . . It had always been there . . .

But, I seldom had the chance to walk towards that revelation
until now.

. . . As the front door was opened for me, I decided to look back . . .
and then I started to cry.

Because that same walkway, which I had been up and down on
thousands of times/that very walkway which had the cul de sac
on either end.

That was the same walkway, which led not to nowhere . . .

. . . But, to Freedom . . .

It Happened One Night (An Erotic Tale)

My sincerest desire should have become a reality . . .

Two beautiful women—one from Africa, the other from China—walked towards me out of the shadows. All I could do was stand there with adolescent like awe. I looked at the African beauty first./Her skin was flawless and colored the darkest of chocolate. She had a small nose, which flared out at the nostrils, and full senuous lips. Her breasts were voluptuous with large, deeply hued areolae . . . The brush of her mound, though coarse was trimmed into a perfect triangle . . .

Her Chinese friend was not as statuesque, but nonetheless breathtaking . . . She had a long mane of hair which fell way past her ass. Her face was absolutely stunning. But, her stomach was especially attractive. For, it only had a tiny dot for a navel. Below that was a thin line of down, which led to a luxurious patch of pubic hair . . ."So which one of us will give you pleasure first?" asked the Chinese beauty. "Her" I said pointing to the African goddess. "My name is Quixoca. Say my name!" she said sternly, yet without anger. "Quixoca" I said in a hypnotized tone. She walked over to me and started touching me everywhere. "You won't be needing these anymore" she said as she helped me out of my shorts. Dropping to her knees, she placed her hands on my thighs and started sucking me deeply/increasing the tempo as she went down and came back up. That's when Chimera, her Chinese friend started kissing me on the neck. She bent down, took one of Quixoca's fingers and placed it in her own mouth. Once it was thouroughly lubricated, Quixoca took it and pushed it inside of me/never breaking the rhythm of her sucking. She pushed her finger in and out until I exploded. The gulping sounds were audible as she swallowed everything I had to offer. It felt so good as I came in her mouth that I started crying, and whispered thank you over and over again . . .

"Now, you have to eat Chimera" Quixoca said sexily. "But, I've never done that before, I don't know how." "Don't worry, she's going to teach you." Chimera laid on the plush carpet and opened her legs invitingly. I knelt down and brought my face to her entrance/inhaling the musky, intoxicating aroma of her sex. I gave her a few tentative kisses there. "No baby, take your hands. open me up, and lick it all over." I did as I was told, and began to lick it with urgency. You know like an ice cream cone that's starting to melt! "Yes baby, just like that." She grabbed the back of my head, and gently held it in place. "Now, take your tongue, and put it inside." Chimera's juices started flowing and I lapped up her nectar like a man dying from thirst . . .

When it was over Quixoca didn't even give me a chance to rest. She straddled me, and slowly, senuously sat on my whole length, while at the same time licking Chimera's wetness from my face. She gingerly pushed her tongue into my mouth. I was so blissed out by her tightness that her tongue just sat there without a friend. She removed her tongue, and whispered in my ear . . ."Give me your tongue as well." Then she raised herself to the head of my manhood, and beautifully lowered herself again. Our lovemaking became so passionate that her vagina started making squishing noises. Faster and faster! Deeper and deeper she rode me until I felt the cum welling up inside! . . .

. . . And, that's when I noticed my hand . . . gliding up and down myself . . . I opened my eyes and realized that I was in my prison cell/masturbating for at least the the hundreth time this week . . .

But, damn . . . wasn't that shit good for ya'll too?

A Poem For The Erudite

A poem for the erudite, it sure will be hot

Take the time out to listen, rubbish it's not

Straight from the life of a perspicacious young man

Try and comprehend it, I sure hope you can

There's a lot I can tell you, but I'll make it laconic . . .

Words to astound, it works like a tonic

But, it all isn't good, I'm sure you'll agree

I robbed to support crack, went on a spree

Nonetheless, I must tell you about erstwhile things

About cause and "affect" and what it all brings

It started with punishment, and led to abuse

Stomped, punched, and kicked like a piece of refuse

That was at home, a total nightmare

Told my story to many/few seemed to care

Yet, at school it was different, totally contraire

There were many happy times, but in all they were rare

Still, to escape from my father—a partial reprieve

An escape so traumatic you can hardly conceive

Fascinated by study, entwined in my thought

Trying to achieve/ knowledge I sought

Then came junior high school, another hill to climb
Still being abused . . . now etched deep in my mind

Then came the reefer, then came the coke

Life became heavy, like being grasped with a choke

Playing hooky from school to hang on the "Deuce
Leaving sadness behind/youth on the loose

Coming home at all hours, high on the drugs
Fending off admonishment . . . not verbally with shrugs

Now, we come to the part of my crack addiction
On a mission to Scotty . . . incarceration/great friction

On a mission five years, retaining intelligent potential
Well, I couldn't lose everything/the mind is essential

But, through all this in jail, you can't know my chagrin
For nothing egregious, no unredeemable sin

Still, remember I told you about cause and "affect"?
Recalled in my poem, I helped you reflect

Being abused was profound, a real heartache
There's been many times I thought . . . my life I would take

But, instead I turned to crack, searching in vain
I know to crack you say, how gravely inane!

Yet, there's a moral to this story/my life in review

I was abused and kicked crack . . . and you can kick too!

Nevertheless, I still believed

I held on tight through doubing voices, the peace I found can't be conceived.

A dead man's hand—two strikes—and snake eyes/
. . . Nevertheless, I Still Believed.

Locked away for many seasons/a grueling, lonely ten year stretch.

Indelible marks of pain and suffering within my soul were deeply etched.

Finally home, I walked uprightly, yet, many sorrows would soon arise.

Homeless people still slept on subways/ the love they lacked seen in their eyes.

Pedophiles did things to children, some were N, Y, P, and D.

I stayed up nights/my spirit questioned, how heinous things like this could be.

On Christopher Street, the trannies younger/ I could've sworn that one was ten.

Right up the block, a boy named Michael, who turned his tricks with older men.

The cell phone craze made me disgusted, to be seen their one desire.

Branded hands and numbered foreheads . . . bogged down in
New World Order's mire.

This country cares for poor Iraqis, for truth and freedom, our soildiers toil.

Patriotism by me regarded, still, I know it's about the oil.

So many emotions overwhelmed me . . . the tears I needed were not supplied.

It seemed that life had much more meaning, when this man spent years inside.

Then my health, which I thought was stable, began to slowly fall apart.

A blocked valve, my beat irregular . . . an aneurysm was in my heart.

Bypass surgery, a long recovery; I felt defeated down in my core.

Yes, there was weakness and thoughts of suicide, because I'd been through this before.

Without Faith I cannot please Him/my will to live replied "agreed."

Severe tests of mind and body.

. . . Nevertheless, I Still Believed . . .

"I AM"

I AM the voice of erstwhile nations

Mali
Ghana and
Songhai

I AM the river of all their sorrows
because their well has now gone dry

I AM
Africa

I AM Wisdom
The one who gave the world its seed

I AM the slave who broke his chains . . .
. . . behind their backs I learned to read

I AM the sound of children weeping
without guidance
Hope
or
Love

I AM their Keeper, I AM compassion
I AM their strength sent from above

I AM the echo of Blackmen's protests
I AM Dark Hued, Caramel, and Tan

I AM a scholar and not inferior . . .
. . . I AM more than "three fifths" a man!

I AM the Sun, the Moon, the Galaxy
I AM the Dawn that brings the Light

I AM the eagle in all its glory
I AM the thought that takes to flight

I AM Maya, Brooks, and Sanchez
I AM the spark that lights the fuse

I AM the Dream that's reached fruition
I AM Woodson, Shabazz, and Hughes

I AM words that are not yet spoken
I AM all of the writers that go unheard

I AM their Spirit, I AM fulfillment . . .

..I AM..

A mixture of conscious stirred

I've Written

I've written verse of strife and struggle, the young one's angst that's locked inside.

I've written words of parents weeping, which stems from teenage suicide.

I've written things on the New World Order/how selfish greed has taken toll.

I've written poems that make me hated, yet, Thoughts
Of Peace Shall Make Us Whole.

I've written songs of Y's and X'ers/murdered kids outlined in chalk.

High corruption—masonic presidents . . . if White House walls could talk.

I've written ryhme on a perverted father, who loved his daughter in a sordid way.

She had a child who was her brother . . .
. . . **Ten Different Shades Of** Gray.

I've written verses on Jews and Arabs/racial bonding—democracy.

I've written it clearly, they're both related, but that Their Eyes Refuse To See.

On the beauty of Brotherhood I've also written, with poignant words I did expound.

I've written a poem which posed a question . . .
. . . Where Then Can Love Be Found?

I've written lines on stress and anguish; From Salted
Tears All Eyes Will Sting.

Still, the next verse had a blessing . . . . But, The Birds No Less Will Sing.

I've written stanzas on 9/11, yet, my quatrain contained much more.

Lost city kids made up Ground Zero, and I named it Metaphor.

I've written pieces on crime with panic, how in every country you see its traces.

I've written of lands with few tomorrows . . . . Where Children's
Ragdolls Hide Their Faces.

I've wriiten memoirs of life in prison, the time I lost can't be conceived.

I've written that Faith in God sustained me in
Nevertheless, I Still Believed.

I've written sweet words on Joy and Goodness, with hopes that evil will not remain.

I've written deep lyrics on every topic . . .
. . . so that others can feel my pain . . .

Sometimes

Sometimes . . . I feel as if I were stillborn . . .
Devoid of a future
Bereft of hope
A deformed fetus, which never left its mother's womb/
routinely scraped out of a cavity like so much detritus,
and then forgotten

Sometimes . . . I feel naked in a world which
idolizes clothing
This man's raiment who suffers is loneliness/
an ill—fitting garment of despair

Sutures on the Pai Hui, which I've loosed long ago.
once again tigthen my skull like a vise . . .
For, I cannot fathom why there is so much violence,
when we all claim to be civilized

Orbs covered by glasses of red/but, the red
that I see is not roseate - it is vermilion -
the color of blood . . .

The blood of minorities/the blood of those ethnically cleansed -

The blood of innocent children destroyed
by heartless predators and abusers

. . . The Blood of the Son Of God, who has many names,
yet has no face . . . The Blood Of The Lamb

. . . I am The Voice Of One Crying In The Wilderness . . .

Still, who will dare to straighten the paths
made crooked by an evil empire?

They see not—they hear not— they are not
Can you unravel this mystery? . . .

The evil empire can only be seen by those with
Spiritual Eyes/though their Masonic symbols are everywhere

It's on the back of a dollar bill
Can you see it? . . .

I thought not, because greed and blindness
go hand in hand

Nonetheless, at the close of the day,
when my meditations are over - when my tears
have all been spent - when my very soul is at an end . . .

. . . Then . . .

I fully realize that I am vulnerable/just barely capable
of hanging on . . .

It is then that I'm certain that I'm merely a child

. . . who needs to be found . . .

. . . Sometimes . . .

The Ten Mouthfuls

It's been several months since this incident occurred. Yet, in my heart of hearts, I feel compelled to write about it. Don't think that I'm a writer. I'm not. Actually, I'm homeless. Nonetheless, even though I'm not a writer. And, even though I'm homeless. I feel confident that I can compose this story in such a way that even the most callous person will be humbled.

It was a cold and wet, winter weeknight and I was miserable. The windchill made it feel like minus twenty. Manhattan streets were so devoid of passersby, that it looked like a scene right out of Escape From New York. So, of course panhandling didn't pan out this night. Pardon the pun. Despite the negatives, I continued my hustle into the early morning hours. By three o clock though, the wind made me a believer and I started walking towards Penn Station before I froze to death. The course to my destination would be the same. Walk along Eigthth Avenue, taking in the all too familiar boring buildings and businesses. Only this morning, I would be walking at a much faster pace. I got to the large subway gratings alongside Penn Station, and did as I always did. Instead of walking across them, I stepped to my left and walked past them.

Surprisingly, the escalator wasn't working, so I walked down the two short flights. On past the plexiglass enclosed waiting area I walked, until I reached the second flight of escalators in what I'll call the foyer. This is the area that I sleep in. Right under the escalator. Going to sleep in Penn Station is an exercise in trepidation and calm. Trepidation because there's always the police bothering us. Then there's the occassional demented homeless person, and teenagers looking for trouble. Calm because it might take time to fall asleep just from the stresses of being homeless. Finally, after opening my eyes to any noises, real or imagined. I fell into an uneasy, but fitful sleep.

Hunger pains jolted me awake at 8am. I was elated and quite shocked that I got to sleep for almost five hours. What was disheartening was the fact that I would soon have to pound the pavement panhandling in the gelid, morning air. Then, there was my hunger. Which by now was too profound to ignore. If it's true that a person's stomach speaks to them when they're hungry. Mine was speaking to me in ten different languages at once. Still under the escalators, I put my arms above my head and stretched. Then, I scanned the ground around me. Making sure that my few, precious belongings were still there. And, that's when I saw it! Sitting next to my leg was a styrofoam container. You know the ones you get when you go to a Chinese restaurant.

Just thinking about what culinary delights the container held had my mouth watering. I looked around nervously, as if someone would come and claim their food. When I was sure that I was just being paranoid, I picked up the container, and opened it expectantly. Well, my happiness quickly dissolved into depair. The sumptuous banquet that I hoped to find was nothing more than several, miserable mouthfuls. I actually started to cry thinking about the creep, who was probably laughing somewhere with morbid pleasure about leaving a homeless person a corner of food. My first intention was to throw the tray, against the escalator wall. A cooler head prevailed though, and I opted for a more gentler recourse. I merely pushed the tray a few inches away from me. And, then I started to brood. When I stopped feeling sorry for myself, I made the motions as if I were about to stand up. But, my reality brought me back to reality if you understand my meaning. My reality was that I was still hungry. The reality beyond my hunger was that the tray, with its exiguous contents was still on the floor.

I turned to my right and sneered at the tray. Nonetheless, my decision was made. I picked up the tray, opened it, and shoveled two spoonfuls into my mouth. My stomach was so relieved to be getting some attention, that my eyes closed in remembrance. I remembered the look of sheer bliss on Tom Hank's face in the movie Castaway, when he speared that fish, cooked it, and took that initial taste. The look of Tom Hanks eating after being bereft of food for so long? . . . . Priceless.

I opened my eyes, and got ready to eat some more of the Middle Eastern dish of spicy rice, grilled, chopped vegetables, and white sauce. But, it was all gone. I guess during my reverie, I forgot how little there was and unknowingly continued to eat. With the anger all but gone and my hunger pains subsided. I leaned back against the escalator wall and drifted into thought. I knew that I learned a valuable lesson from this experience. I realized that this wasn't about the food, or lack thereof. It wasn't even about the person who left it. It was about me being homeless and having very little. About me receiving even less than a little in that styrofoam tray. In retrospect though, those few mouthfuls were probably more gratifying than any feast I could have ever imagined. Because on that day, yes, at that moment in my sojourn through this life. I learned to be thankful for even the smallest of blessings . . . **The Lesson Of The Ten Mouthfuls.**

Poeta Nascitur Nonfit

A Poet Is Born
Not Made